fast thinking.
finding facts

C000070721

PEARSON EDUCATION LIMITED

Head Office:
Edinburgh Gate
Harlow CM20 2JE
Tel: +44 (0)1279 623623
Fax: +44 (0)1279 431059

London Office:
128 Long Acre
London WC2E 9AN
Tel: +44 (0)20 7447 2000
Fax: +44 (0)20 7240 5771
Website: www.business-minds.com

First published in Great Britain in 2001

© Pearson Education Limited 2001

The right of Richard Templar to be identified as Author
of this Work has been asserted by him in accordance
with the Copyright, Designs and Patents Act 1988.

ISBN 0 273 65319 9

British Library Cataloguing in Publication Data
A CIP catalogue record for this book can be obtained from the British Library

10 9 8 7 6 5 4 3 2 1

Typeset by Pantek Arts Ltd, Maidstone, Kent.
Printed and bound in Great Britain by Ashford Colour Press, Hampshire.

The Publishers' policy is to use paper manufactured from sustainable forests.

2

fast
thinking:
finding
facts

- ▶ **support your case**
- ▶ **find smart quotes**
- ▶ **exploit the internet**

by Richard Templar

contents

introduction

So, you've managed somehow to find a few scant hours to write your proposal or report, or prepare your presentation and now you realise that you're going to have to spend half of it frantically searching for data to back up your arguments. How on earth are you going to find so many facts in so little time? You don't even have time to get up from your desk and walk to the filing cabinet, let alone get down to the library or the nearest decent newsagent. And the Internet ... well, once you log on your computer just mutates into a machine that eats time.

Maybe you're lucky and you need just one key fact with which to stun the opposition at a vital meeting. Then again, maybe the meeting is only ten minutes away. Not so lucky, then. Or perhaps your boss wants the information for a presentation this afternoon and has just thrown a list of data at you and told you to come up with the answers by lunchtime.

Whatever the reason, you need facts and you need them fast. Well, help is at hand. This book is about getting hold of vital, relevant information quickly and accurately. In fact, without even having to leave the building. No more spending hours on the Net cruising when you should be surfing. It will all be explained clearly and simply.

This book is about finding facts fast. It does exactly what it says on the cover. It will give you:

 Tips for getting away with only the data you really need

 Shortcuts for locating data as fast as possible, and

 Checklists for making sure you have every option covered.

… all put together clearly and simply. And short enough to read fast, of course.

This book will assume that you have a day or two at most to get your facts, but you'll find a section at the back which deals with the tighter deadline of a couple of hours. And there's even a getting-the-facts-instantly section too.

So take a deep breath, and roll up those sleeves. We've got some work to do and there's no time for sleeping. We are thinking at the speed of life.

This book will take you through the key stages of finding facts fast:

1   Set your objective before you do anything else. It keeps you focused and prevents you getting side-tracked down blind alleys.

2   Next, you need to know exactly what information you're searching for, so we'll look at the questions you need to ask yourself before you begin.

3   Where are you going to go for these facts? You're pushed for time, but there's still likely to be a choice of sources. You need to make the right choice first time – you can't afford to go the long way round when there's a shorter route to the same data.

4   If you're serious about finding data, you need to know how to use the Internet. It's quick, easy, cheap, and available 24 hours a day (good news if you're still up working at three in the morning). It is also, however, a minefield: unreliable in parts and extremely large. You could get lost if you didn't have this *Fast Thinking* guide at your elbow as an excellent route map and encouraging companion.

5   The final stage is verifying your facts. OK, so you've collected your information, but how reliable is it? And how much junk can the Internet throw up? (Answer: More than you think.) You need to verify your facts and make sure their accuracy is unquestionable.

You'll also find a couple of useful chapters to read when you have time:

- 'fast but not now': a guide to the best software and hardware for finding facts now, from fast modems to mirror sites. Update your system ready for next time, and you'll be able to lay your hands on all that cyber-data even faster.
- 'smart but not fast': a guide to other valuable sources of information which you don't have time for today, but which could save you time in the future if you have a longer lead time to get them rolling.

You need to make the right choice first time – you can't afford to go the long way round when there's a shorter route to the same dataa

fast thinking gambles

Of course you need more time to get these facts. Of course, in an ideal world, you wouldn't have a million and one other things to do at the same time. But hey, wake up and smell the coffee. It ain't an ideal world. No good blubbing; let's get on with it. This book will give you all the help you need given the tight deadline, but it's always some kind of gamble:

- ► You won't have time to verify all the facts as accurately as you might like to. We'll give you the key pointers to identifying reliable sources – and unreliable ones, of course – but this means taking some facts on trust.

- ► You may not have time to collect all the facts you need. Perhaps you'd like to round up 20 facts to support your case, but you may have to be content with only half a dozen key facts – just enough to get you out of trouble this time.

- ► Some information simply isn't available in the time you have. Maybe you don't have time to trek off to the library, or the one person who knows the answer is out of the office until next week.

 Maybe the information is out there, but at a price. And you haven't time to get clearance for exceeding the budget.

All that said, you can certainly keep yourself out of trouble with this book at your side. But for added reassurance next time, and to get hold of the best data around, clear yourself more time if it's humanly possible.

But for added reassurance next time, and to get hold of the best data around, clear yourself more time if it's humanly possible

1 your objective

I know you're on the verge of panic, but just stop and think for a moment. It will save you a huge amount of time in the long run, I promise. You need to think about what it is you're really trying to achieve.

The facts you want to find are simply a means to an end, not an end in themselves. What are you going to do with the information once you've found it? You're going to use it, that's what. So your starting point is to identify what you want the facts *for* – without this you can't hope to identify which facts you need.

The odds are that you need this information for one of three purposes:

1 to back up your arguments and persuade people to accept your proposal, your presentation or your standpoint at an imminent meeting

2 to include in a report you've been asked to write in order to add credibility to it

3 to enable you to make a decision.

By far the most frequent of these is the first one. If you're this pressed for time, and it's this important, the odds are you're trying to produce facts which will support your case and persuade a customer, colleague or boss to adopt your proposal. What's more, if you're putting together a proposal or presentation, you may have to find a lot of facts – and in a hurry, too.

So you should begin by identifying the objective of the overall proposal you are making (whether you're writing it, presenting it or putting it across at a meeting). This will help you focus on what the facts you are looking for will need to achieve. And it will help you save time, as you'll see.

SETTING YOUR OVERALL OBJECTIVE

This thought process should take you only a few moments, but will help hugely in setting a clear objective. Suppose you are proposing to your board that staffing levels in your department be increased. A statement of your aim might be simply: *to persuade the board to increase staffing levels in the department.* But the more detail you add, the more helpful your objective will be.

It's just like planning a journey: you need to decide not only where you are going, but also how you are going to get there. In other words, what are the main requirements of your journey? Speed? Plenty of interesting stop-offs on the way? Low fuel consumption? A convenient place to stop for lunch? Flesh out the objective a little more. Here's a fresh version: *to persuade the board that increased staffing levels in the department would be more productive.*

Now we're getting somewhere. But we need to be still more specific. What does 'more productive' mean? More cost-effective? Or will it generate more income? Or speed up the system? What benefit are you trying to sell to your board: what turns them on? Cutting costs? Increasing output? Improving customer service? Operating a faster system?

OK, let's try again: *to persuade the board that increased staffing levels in the department would improve customer service and generate more income than it would cost.* That's more like it. You've thought

thinking smart

THIRD TIME LUCKY

It often takes three stages to set a clear objective. Identify the broad objective first, then state a broad reason why your reader or listener should accept it, and finally make the reason more specific. For example:

1 persuade the board to up staffing levels
2 to make the department more productive
3 in terms of customer service and income/cost balance.

about who the proposal is for and what they want to hear, and you've given yourself an objective that tells you where you're going and the key elements to focus on en route.

So that's your one-sentence objective. It should have taken you only a few moments to write, but you're going to be referring to it frequently over the next few hours.

USING YOUR OBJECTIVE

This objective helps you to focus on the facts you most need: the ones which further your overall objective. Suppose you have dozens of points you'd like to support with facts, but not enough time to dig them all out. Which do you spend time on? In the case of our last example, the ones which demonstrate that additional staffing will:

- ▶ **improve customer service**
- ▶ **generate more income than it will cost.**

So don't get bogged down in dragging out data on past staffing levels, or facts which show that increased staffing will speed up admin procedures. If time is short, concentrate on the data which support your overall objective. If you have the luxury of time left over (when did that last happen?) *then* you can dig out additional information.

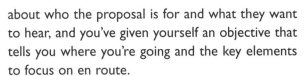

You need to decide not only where you are going, but also how you are going to get there

CLOCKING OFF

If you have time to find more than the absolutely essential facts – congratulations. But your objective is still valuable. It is very easy (especially if you use the Internet) to get hung up on trying to find one particular but highly elusive piece of information. This can waste hours. You could set yourself a time limit, determined by how much time you have. If data do not directly support the overall objective, you'll give up if you haven't located the information within, say, ten minutes.

AN OBJECTIVE FOR EACH FACT

Don't panic: setting an objective for each fact isn't going to take hours. It's just a matter of how you approach it. Suppose you want your board of directors to accept your proposal to introduce a new production system incorporating the recently developed jertain-based process. You need to back up your claim that jertains are much more cost-efficient to run than the old-style wockets. And you're lucky here – you remember reading a report in one of the trade publications about this not long ago. So all you have to do is dig out the article and you've got what you need.

Two hours later, you still can't track down the article you want. It would help if you could remember which publication it was in, but you can't.

You've fallen into a classic trap here: you've got hung up on the *fact*, instead of focusing on the *objective*. The fact, remember, is only a means to an end. And the end purpose was to demonstrate that jertains are more cost-efficient than wockets. But if you keep your eye on the objective, you'll realise that there is more than one way of proving this point.

You could, for example, contact both manufacturers and ask them each to fax or e-mail you the relevant, verified data. Then you can make the comparison yourself. Or you could search the Net for any relevant reports on the subject.

There is usually more than one way to make your point, and you need to focus on what you're trying to achieve in order to pick the fastest approach that will do the trick. And you do that by setting a mini-objective for each fact, such as: *to demonstrate that jertains are more cost-efficient than wockets.*

 thinking smart

ASK YOURSELF

If you have any difficulty working out what your mini-objective is, simply ask yourself a question: 'What am I trying to prove?'

Armed with your overall objective, and mini-objectives for each point you want to back up with facts, you can approach your fact finding in a far more focused way, and you have a framework to stop yourself wasting time on unnecessary detail.

◀◀ for next time

If you are writing a proposal or report, preparing a presentation, or making a key decision, you should already have set the objective for this. (You might like to read the relevant books in this series: *Fast Thinking: Proposal*, *Fast Thinking: Presentation* and *Fast Thinking: Decision*.) This gives you your overall objective for finding facts.

Armed with this, you can make yourself a quick list of all the points you would like to support with hard data and put them in priority order, according to how closely they fit the overall objective. Draw a line below the facts which directly further the overall objective: anything above this line is essential information. Anything below it is desirable but not essential. Then simply work through the list, until you run out of time. You can still set yourself a time limit for each fact, as we saw earlier, and also for each mini-objective.

Armed with your overall objective, and mini-objectives for each point you can approach your fact finding in a far more focused way

2 getting your facts straight

OK, so you've set your objective and you are now ready to get out there and find what you want. But hold on. Do you know where to go? And what you are looking for? Take a little time – and I know you don't have much to spare but this is important – to think clearly about what it is you are researching.

ASKING QUESTIONS

If you know *exactly* what it is you are looking for – fine. But if not then ask a few questions first. When you need to know something ask yourself exactly what it is you are researching. Better to spend five minutes thinking at the beginning than wasting two days later on. If this research is for your own proposal or report then just sit down and ask yourself these few key questions before rushing out there:

▶ **What sort of fact is it?**

▶ **Who is it for?**

- (▶) **What will it cost?**
- (▶) **How much data can I handle?**

We will quickly nip through these questions so you have some guidelines before rushing off and wasting time.

What sort of fact is it?

Facts can be broadly divided up into three categories:

- (▶) *Hard facts.* These are things such as historical facts – things that have happened and are well documented.
- (▶) *Data.* This is really a sub-set of hard facts but it is the sort of numerical information you might need, such as statistics, financial information, numerical data, scientific information, that sort of thing.
- (▶) *Views and opinions.* Perhaps not technically facts but relevant nevertheless. For instance you might need, to know that 78 per cent of people consider facts to be essential to good research – that's their opinion anyway but it is a fact: that's what they think.

Who is it for?

Important one this, as it isn't the *user* of the fact that is important but the end customer, so to speak. You may be the user – the researcher – and you may think the fact is for you. But it isn't. It is for whoever the report or proposal or presentation you are including it in is for – they are the customer. You have to bear them in mind. It is imperative that you know who your customer is and which way to go.

Sometimes you *may* be the end customer. Perhaps you have to make an important decision and you need the relevant facts to make that

thinking smart

THINK LATERALLY

Don't get bogged down in always using the same avenue of research. The smart manager will chop and change as the circumstances change. You might usually go to the Internet for information, but this time there might be quicker, slicker sources. Take a moment to consider if you aren't using one source from habit rather than expediency.

thinking smart

SHOTGUNS AND PISTOLS

The smart manager will know that one clear, well-presented fact that is well documented and verified might swing the balance in their favour considerably more than a whole range of facts badly researched and lacking in authority. Having said that, the shotgun approach *may* be more effective: smart managers choose their weapon carefully!

decision. In which case you will have to be both judge and jury, so to speak. You will have to tailor your search to your own specific needs.

What will it cost?

The Internet, on the whole, is a free source of facts, but they may not be either verifiable or accurate. Some site owners – especially the more reliable ones – may well have to be reimbursed for their trouble.

Some organisations charge for information: trade bodies, magazines and newspapers for archived articles.

How much data can I handle?

How much data can you handle physically? For instance, you may need to read and understand a 50-page document on the Internet just to find out one

thinking fast

PHONE A FRIEND
One well-placed phone call to someone in the know can save you an awful lot of time and effort. Before you log on take the time to think about who might have this information. Asking a friend takes but a second but might save you a lot of time in the long run. If they don't know the answer, they may know someone who does.

WHO'S BEEN HERE BEFORE?

The smart-thinking manager will look at who might have had or needed this information before. Why waste time and effort researching facts when someone might have done all the donkey work for you? Take a moment or two to think about possible fact users that have gone before you. This might be previous company reports, sales statistics, financial documents, even books written on the subject.

CHECK YOUR FACTS

Before adding a fact to any document always ask yourself: 'If asked to justify or verify this fact, can I?' If you can't then don't put it in. Don't try to wing it: you'll get caught out, if not this time then next time for sure. Always have the back-up information to hand so you don't have to memorise vast chunks of data but can quote your sources at the flip of a page.

tiny piece of data. And on screen at that. Are you up to it? Can you read fast and accurately? Can your computer handle such vast amounts of information? Have you got time to read it all? We will look at ways of speeding all this up later but bear in mind when we first set off to hunt down our fact that we must be ready for information overload – and have contingency plans to deal with it.

GET A CLEAR BRIEFING

If someone else has asked you to research these facts, you will need to know how many, how big, how detailed. For instance, you might be asked for the number of washing machines sold in Germany in 1998. Fine and off you go. But before you waste time ask your boss a few other questions, such as:

- ▶ **New or second-hand or both?**
- ▶ **Just German machines or all makes?**
- ▶ **Imports or only home sales?**
- ▶ **Retail or wholesale?**
- ▶ **Include exports?**
- ▶ **Domestic or industrial?**
- ▶ **Home sales or trade sales or both?**

Each one of these questions can refine your search and if you hadn't asked you may well be off on the wrong trail altogether. Once you have asked you might be told that the only information required is for domestic sales through retail outlets for home use of new German machines – there, that simplified things, didn't it?

Now let's get on with finding facts for real.

for next time

When you are planning your next report or presentation or proposal, check what facts you are going to need to support your case or argument. And check what facts you need well in advance of needing them. This will give you much more time to collect them and also allow time for emergencies. It's simply no good to wait to the last minute to log onto the Internet for a few quick relevant facts only to find your server is down or your computer is crashing or your phone line is out of action. The smart manager plans in advance and leaves nothing to the last minute if they can help it.

As soon as you know there is a report or presentation to do, start collecting facts: cut out articles from newspapers that may be relevant. These things take only a second but can prove very valuable at the last minute. If you don't need them then you haven't lost much at all.

Use key questions to refine your search before you start

3 your options

OK, so time is getting on and we haven't even switched on the computer yet. We looked briefly in the last chapter at the sort of information you might be likely to need. Next, where can you get it from? Look at your requirements and decide what sort of facts you need. This makes it easier to determine your source.

WHERE CAN I FIND IT?

For most people the top of the list will be the Internet but it really depends on the type of facts you are looking for. The Internet is a vast virtual library of information that is unbelievably diverse, covering any and every topic imaginable. But it also has its drawbacks:

▶ It can eat up time you just don't have.

▶ Some of the information is quite deliberately biased or incorrect.

▶ It is too big to use for research unless you really know what you are doing (which you will do by the time you've finished reading this book).

- (▶) It provides distractions and dead ends that will entangle and ensnare you.

Probably the best source of information is the Internet, but before you log on don't discount other sources such as:

- (▶) accountants' reports, audited accounts and financial reports, stock market reports, treasury statements
- (▶) biographers and historians
- (▶) company library and company reports, internal records, minutes of meetings
- (▶) a friend, colleague or expert
- (▶) financial journals, digests, magazines, manuals, newspaper archives, pamphlets, periodicals, scientific periodicals, magazines
- (▶) publishers
- (▶) reference and university libraries (they may be online)
- (▶) competitor information
- (▶) resource directories
- (▶) trade associations and professional bodies

You probably don't have time to leave the building, but you may be surprised at what you can find out with a quick phone call, fax or e-mail to any of these sources.

The Internet is a vast virtual library of information that is unbelievably diverse, covering any and every topic imaginable

For instance, you might need to know who supplies your competitor with the three-inch widgets that they fit in their giggle pins for their revolving jertains. You could spend ages on the Internet cruising and surfing and getting side-tracked. A quick trip to your sales office, however, might give you a copy of your competitor's latest leaflet proclaiming in large bold type **'and with the new unbeatable three-inch widget from Pearson Industrial!'** See, I told you this stuff was easy.

Or you might need the investment value of Georgian silver over the last 200 years. And whereas you could eventually find this on the Internet after a great deal of searching, a quick

thinking smart

BEING A DETECTIVE

Smart managers regard themselves more like a detective than a researcher – they look for clues as to where they might find the information, they follow up leads, they root around, they follow hunches and their nose, they ferret out information others might miss, they aren't afraid to phone up an expert or a friend, they have an uncanny sense of where information might lurk. They take research to a new and interesting dimension.

USE THE EXPERTS

Whatever fact you need to know, there will be someone who regards this fact highly. For you it is just ammunition for a report or proposal but for some anorak somewhere it is their life and blood. Find them and ask what you need to know. They will be flattered to be asked and invariably will part with the information free of charge. These people don't know things because it is their business but because they study them out of interest.

phone call to an antique dealer specialising in Georgian silver may well turn up trumps. It's the sort of information they may well have merely by chance – because they are interested in all aspects of their business.

If you need to research public opinion – or anyone's opinions come to that – then check the sources just given. For instance, to back up your argument you might like to show, from market research surveys, that **88** per cent of people, when asked for a preference, declared that they thought having a jertain in the home was a good idea and they would definitely buy one if the price was right. Simply brilliant if you are trying to persuade your board to branch out into the home jertain market.

Probably the best source of information is the Internet, but before you log on don't discount other sources

If you are researching opinions then don't forget: politics, advice, counselling, warnings, government positions, conventions, guidelines, management topics and regulations. For instance, you might want to know if it is feasible, or even considered ethical, to keep jertains in the domestic environment without a licence. This is still a fact – not data, not a hard fact, but a view, a position, an opinion, a guideline.

So where do we get this stuff from? Well, for public opinion obviously market research, although this is limited when you're up against the clock (when time is less tight, see 'smart but not fast', page 76). Then there are loads of government offices simply dying to give out juicy titbits of information to those who ask.

THE OUTERNET

You could always subscribe to an Internet information database if this would throw up the results you

thinking smart

E-MAIL ROUND ROBIN

You can always send a round robin e-mail to a number of colleagues or friends or experts asking their advice as to where to go for certain information. They may well already have it or could certainly point you in the right direction.

wanted. Basically, these are online research agencies with computerised facilities. They are known as pure knowledge databases or knowledge indexes and are part of the Outernet – outside the Internet for fee-paying customers. You have to pay for them but they are reliable and trustworthy sources. You can usually subscribe directly online using a valid credit card and have instant access.

You get what you pay for

Unlike the Internet where it is all free and thus anyone can post anything they want including illegal, misleading, faked, hoaxed and silly information – and they do, believe me – the Outernet is based pretty much on a 'you get what you pay for' sort of basis. These databases are selling data so they are updated very frequently – after all, their reputation depends on their data being accurate. They would go out of business fast if they weren't reliable.

A lot of these are American and they work by charging you a yearly subscription (around £50 per annum) and then you pay a per hour fee while you are online. This can range from as low as £10 per hour to as high as £200. Some also charge you if you print out any information – usually around 50p a page. The biggest of these is to be found at

There are loads of government offices simply dying to give out juicy titbits of information to those who ask

http://www.dialog.com/. This isn't a recommendation – merely a fact.

Different data

Beware the fact that most of them are American and the information can sometimes be misleading or very different from ours owing to the different way we handle data and figures; for instance, we are only just beginning to use 'billion' in the same way. Until recently our billion was one million million, whereas the American billion is only one thousand million – could throw your data out by a long way, stuff like that!

for next time

Make yourself acquainted with online newspapers, journals and other publications. Surf when you have a little time to spare – not now. Try:

http://www.publist.com/ This website covers over 150,000 magazines, journals and newsletters, with many links to publishers. It also has pre-launch listings.

http://www.mediafinder.com/ This one covers over 100,000 publications and includes mailing list vendors. It has a user database research section with free search by keyword or category.

http://ajr.newslink.org/ This has coverage of over 3,000 US and 2,000 foreign newspapers and links to campus newspapers.

Make yourself acquainted with online newspapers, journals and other publications. Surf when you have a little time to spare – not now

4 sourcing your facts

Now we know what we need to find out. It's time to switch on, log on and get started. We simply don't have the time to learn about the history of the Internet or how it came to be. All we need to know, and quickly, is that it is a useful tool for us to use for research – and how we can use that tool effectively and fast. Above all fast. We may need to learn some new terms and commands but they will be simple and clearly explained. What we are looking for here is the essence of speed, not a retraining programme in the art of the Internet. We are thinking at the speed of life and need only the barest essentials along our journey.

Until a few years ago researching on the Internet was a bit hit-and-miss. Today it is vast and comprehensive – too vast, some might say. But if you know how to refine your search, you can find what you want. Quickly now: the seconds are ticking away and we have a lot to learn if you are to find these facts to make your presentation or report the best there is and capable of doing exactly what you want – backing up your argument and proving your case.

Let's quickly run through finding facts on the Internet and see if we can track down what you are looking for.

HOT LINKS

If you find a web page you think is relevant, you will also find hotlinks. These jump you to the next site of interest but you can find yourself wandering off course and getting lost. You could follow hotlinks for hours without turning up anything of any use. What you want is a website that lists all the sites relevant to your search. These are known as jumpstations and are put together by:

▶ **businesses**

▶ **interested people**

▶ **universities**

▶ **trade associations**

▶ **libraries.**

USE THE RIGHT BUTTON

If you right-click on a website listed on a jumpstation, you will be given various options including 'open in new window'. Left-click on this option and you will be taken to the website in a new browser window without losing your jumpstation. You can do this as many times as you want. Thus you can have as many windows open as you want. While one is loading you can be reading another. Close any that seem to be of little use.

Add these to your bookmarks if they seem useful. To open any web pages simply left-click on them and you will be taken there. Left-click on your 'back' button to return to the jumpstation. You'll usually find jumpstations listed at the top of search engine pages.

SEARCH ENGINES

Search engines do exactly that – they search for you. They have databases of keywords used on website pages and they will quickly trawl through them to locate any that match your search. You simply type in a word and the search engine will find any sites that use that word. They work by searching out words on the opening page of a website. They often only check the first paragraph or two, so if your keyword doesn't appear until later on you won't be given that page to check. The software that does the checking is known as a spider and spiders check the metatag of a website, which is a series of HTML lines – the title, the address (its URL – uniform resource locator), the description and, most important, the keywords. They also check that the keywords listed for the site agree with what's on the opening page.

The downside of this is that search engines are almost impossible to keep up to date and if you use a common word you will be inundated with sites. Try typing in a simple word like 'facts' at Yahoo! and you will be given some 2,680 sites to look at.

"Quotation marks"

To speed up your search – and speed is of the essence here – add words to your search. The

thinking smart

USING AND CHOOSING SEARCH ENGINES

Don't get bogged down in using only one search engine – your favourite. Always use several as they are all different, have different speeds of search and use differing keywords. Use several such as AltaVista, Yahoo!, Ask Jeeves and Excite – bookmark these to speed up access to them.

more words you add, the greater the chances your search engine will find what you are looking for. But if you use more than one word as a keyword search, remember that you should put those words into double quotation marks "like this" or the search engine will try to search out each word individually.

For instance if you type in *German washing machine manufacturers,* the search engine will find you all sites using the word German, as well as all sites using the word washing, plus sites using the word machine and finally add in all sites including the word manufacturers. It's been done for you:

German washing machine manufacturers – 4,259,712 sites

"German washing machine manufacturers" – 22 sites

Not putting your keywords into quotation marks also throws up some interesting additions. For instance, you don't just get all sites using the word washing in the last example: you also get all the sites using washing in any other context, such as *Washington* – both the place and the president.

Most search engines are free as they collect their revenue from advertising. Some are larger than others – they use more keywords – and some are faster. Remember that no one search engine is ever capable of searching more than around 15 per cent of the Internet. This is why you always need to use more than one. We will look at faster ways of refining your search under Boolean searching on page 43 – go there now if you need to know really urgently.

Search engines worth using (and bear in mind that there are around 350 of them currently) include:

- AltaVista
- Yahoo!
- HotBot
- Snap!
- Google
- Excite
- Lycos
- Direct hit
- Northern Light
- Deja
- GoTo.

To get to them just type in their name plus .com. For instance, to get to AltaVista type in AltaVista.com and you'll be taken there. Don't worry about the exact name as these search engines seem to have all possibilities covered. For instance, you could type:

If you use more than one word as a keyword search, remember that you should put those words into double quotation marks

- ▶ **altavista.com**
- ▶ **AltaVista.com**
- ▶ **Alta Vista.com**
- ▶ **Alta-Vista.com**
- ▶ **alta-vista.com**

… and you'll still be taken there. You can even miss out the .com and you'll get taken there. And don't worry too much even about the spelling – altavist will get you there, as will altivista.

Once at a search engine type in "search engines" to be given more.

METASEARCHES

A metasearch engine is one which searches the search engines. They look through the databases of several search engines at once and report back to you with a list of the results. If you haven't found what you are looking for or need a lot of information then trying a metasearch may pay off, especially if you are looking for a lot of obscure information. The downside of metasearches is that they can be overwhelming – they open up each new search in a new window and do tend to bombard you with information. Good to use when you are really proficient. Also most metasearch engines aren't too happy with the maths or Boolean commands – see later. But you could try:

- ▶ **All4one**
- ▶ **Savvy Search**
- ▶ **Web-search**
- ▶ **Suite101**
- ▶ **Searcha-z**
- ▶ **Cyward**
- ▶ **Matchsite.**

MULTI-SEARCH ENGINES

Basically the same as metasearch engines, except they don't try to combine all the results. Instead they open each result in a new window for you. They still send your search item to a number of search engines but each is displayed individually.

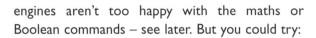

thinking fast

ACRONYMS

If what you are looking for is often known by its acronym then use the Boolean command OR to widen your search. If you need information on NATO then type in both the acronym and the full name: *NATO OR North Atlantic Treaty Organization.*

This can be confusing or time-saving, depending on how many results you get. Multi-search engines are very good at presenting you with new search engines that you might not have tried before. Try:

▶ **Searchspaniel.com**

▶ **Theinfo.com**

SEARCH ENGINES WITH DIRECTORIES

By narrowing down your search you can get a better response. Most search engines will allow you to confine your search, if you want to, to certain key areas or categories of interest, such as:

▶ **health**

▶ **entertainment**

▶ **business**

▶ **companies**

ththth **thinkingsfast**

HYPERLINKED SEARCH ENGINES

Most search engines list other search engines at the bottom of their opening page. If you type in a keyword and fail to get a decent response, simply click on the hyperlinked search engines listed to be taken there; they will begin your search again without your having to retype your keyword/s.

- ▶ travel
- ▶ sport
- ▶ money
- ▶ news
- ▶ jobs
- ▶ people finder
- ▶ real estate.

It makes sense to use one of these directories if you want to exclude data from other areas that may not be relevant. For instance, if you want to research jertains you might like to know which companies import them but you might not want to know anything about their history, development or capabilities. Limiting your search to companies only would throw up relevant data but exclude all the stuff you don't want. Most of the search engines allow you to refine your search in this way but you could do worse than try:

- ▶ Magellan
- ▶ Yahoo!
- ▶ Excite
- ▶ Webcrawler
- ▶ Lycos.

By narrowing down your search you can get a better response

CAPITALS

If what you are looking for is a proper noun then make sure you put it into capitals. If you are looking for Apple computers instead of the apples you eat, make sure you put the capital in for the Apple or you'll be inundated with fruit.

Again no specific endorsement, merely an observation.

WEB RINGS

Once you start surfing you might notice, usually at the bottom of a page, what is known as a web ring. This is a series of very similar sites which have got together to link to each other. One site might not have quite what you are looking for but another, on the same subject, may have exactly what you want. They can be a little time-consuming to follow but are often worth a search if you are looking for detail on a particular subject. For instance, perhaps you need to know a detail about the latest development of fuel-injection systems for jertains. You log on to the official jertain site at jertain.com but that only tells you that a new development has been made. You notice a web ring and click on it. It shows you five other jertain sites including jertaindevelopment.com. Off you go and there is the detail you wanted. You might never have thought to try jertaindevelopment.com but the web ring has taken you there.

ARCHIVES (GOPHERS)

When the Web first started, many universities and library facilities put a lot of text-based information on to it so other similar organisations could browse them. These text-based archives are still out there and can be accessed by anyone. Sometimes a particular bit of information you seek will be lying dormant just waiting for you to reactivate it. Such archives are very similar to encyclopaedia entries – just much more comprehensive and detailed. Use them if you want more information on a particular subject than a reference book or a CD of an encyclopaedia would give you. They are often updated as well, so they will give you up-to-the-minute political stuff as well, as current events.

These sites are known as gopher archives and you might like to search them out at:

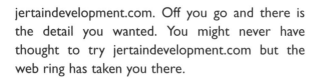

- ▶ **Archie**
- ▶ **Veronica**
- ▶ **Galaxy**
- ▶ **Jughead.**

Sometimes a particular bit of information you seek will be lying dormant just waiting for you to reactivate it

They may be useful, especially if what you want is typical archive material. Gopher archives are not technically part of the Web and if you type a gopher address into your web browser you need to use gopher:// rather than http://. They are best for academic research and anything to do with government offices.

NEWSGROUPS

If you haven't found what you want by now (and you probably will have), then you'll have to widen your search. Out there, in or on the Web (whichever you prefer) there are millions of people. Some of these have similar interests and like to communicate with each other. They do this through newsgroups. Newsgroups deal with very specific topics and exchange views and information freely and successfully. By subscribing to a newsgroup (joining it) you have access to whatever that newsgroup discusses.

You can post a message asking for particular information and receive replies by e-mail. This can be very useful sometimes, as you can gain access to someone who is heavily into a particular subject and as such may even be an expert. You may be inundated with e-mails or, as is more likely, receive only a few which answer your queries.

Vigilant and InReference both allow for keyword searches with the results being sent to you via e-mail. This saves a lot of time having to read every article about items. Both allow filtering so you can specify exactly what you want.

VALIDATING THE INFORMATION

Through newsgroups you can access the latest developments in some pretty fundamental research. You can also be led astray or receive misleading information. With a newsgroup there is no way, except through a sort of sixth sense, in which you can determine the validity of any information you are getting. And a sixth sense might not cut much ice with your readers or audience. Newsgroups, however, can often put you on the right trail of vital information that *can* be validated.

Most servers (this is the medium through which you access the Internet yourself; they serve you and you are their client) will have a list of newsgroups; you could try searching the search engines, or Deja News is a specific newsgroup search engine.

There are over 24,000 newsgroups currently. That's over 24,000 different subject areas – good for research. Always visit a newsgroup's FAQ – frequently asked questions – page first to see if the sort of thing you are looking for is being talked about within the newsgroup, as some have misleading titles and you might have accidentally stumbled into the wrong place.

REFINING YOUR SEARCH

Search engines work by looking for keywords in the title (usually) page of a website. They work by searching through words. Logically then, if you give them more words to search they are more likely to come up trumps for you. We looked earlier at the example of German washing machine manufacturers and how to put this search into quotation marks; well, there are a lot of other ways of refining your search. The two principal methods are known as maths and Boolean. Maths works by inserting symbols such as + or − into your request. Boolean works by inserting the words AND, NOT, NEAR and OR.

MATHS SEARCHES

The more specific your search, the more likely you are to come up with good, useful material − and quicker, which is what we are really interested in. By adding in a maths symbol you refine your search in great detail. Perhaps you want to know all about car manufacturers. Typing in *cars* would give you a lot of pages including ones on racing cars, kit cars,

THE + SYMBOL

Use the + symbol when you want to narrow your search down: it is useful when you're being overwhelmed with information. You can refine your search to anything you want. For instance, if you want to search out a Bogart movie such as *Casablanca*, type in *Bogart + Casablanca* and you'll omit any pages which might give you his other films, as well as omitting any pages which give you biographies, fan clubs or well-known quotations, sites selling photos and posters, and even sites selling the T-shirt.

repairing cars, spraying cars and driving cars. Typing in *manufacturers* would give you a lot as well – and include a lot of manufacturers of other things such as washing machines. But both would contain irrelevant information which you would waste time sifting through.

Typing in *"car manufacturers"* would throw up only pages which use that exact phrase. By typing in *car +manufacturers* you would get only pages which used both words – not necessarily next to each other but on the same page. The more + symbols you put in, the narrower your search becomes. For instance, *car +manufacturers +Europe* would exclude all manufacturers from other places

The more specific your search the more likely you are to come up with good, useful material as well as manufacturers of washing machines or anything else.

You should use the – (minus) symbol when you want to *exclude* specific information. For instance, you might like to know about European car manufacturers but not Volkswagen or BMW as you already have enough information on them. So you would type in *car +manufacturers +Europe –Volkswagen –BMW*. That should omit anything to do with Volkswagen or BMW.

thinking smart

CLOSE UP THE GAPS

Make sure that when you are typing in maths commands (+, –) you place these symbols next to the word which refines your search and don't leave a space. It should be *Shakespeare +Othello*, not *Shakespeare + Othello*.

thinking smart

KNOWING THE DIFFERENCE

The plus and minus symbols narrow your search down to pages which contain the information you want but not necessarily in any set order. Quotation marks narrow your search down to a specific phrase as it appears on a web page.

Boolean searches

Boolean searches are used by many professional researchers, although they are, as often as not, being replaced by maths searches these days. They are still extremely useful and can speed up your search considerably. Boolean searches work by allowing you to substitute one word for another without having to search twice. For instance, you might like to know about hair colouring. You can type in *blonde OR* blond and get pages listing either or both.

Most major search engines allow the use of OR (except Google because it does it automatically).

If you want to tie in two words, you use AND. For instance, if you want to find sites that cover both Tony Blair and Gordon Brown, type in *Blair AND Brown*.

thinking smart

WATCH YOUR LANGUAGE!

If your word search includes any of the four words used in Boolean searching then make sure you place them in quotation marks or you will confuse your search engine. For instance, you might be looking for references to the book *Sons and Lovers*. If you type this in, you will get pages on sons and pages on lovers but you might not get any pages listing the book you want. Instead type in "Sons and Lovers" and you will get your result.

Most if not all major search engines allow the use of AND, and in those that don't you can substitute + instead and it will do the same job.

Likewise Boolean searches allow you to omit certain sites. In the example about British politicians you might like to have sites for Tony Blair only and ignore any mentioning both. Type in *Blair NOT Brown.*

All major search engines support the NOT command except Google and Look Smart but they will allow the − symbol instead.

If you want to find pages which have two words close to each other then you use the NEAR command. For instance, *car NEAR manufacturers* will refine your search considerably. Most major search engines have their own convention as to what NEAR means. In AltaVista it means within 10 words, in WebCrawler within two words and in Lycos within 25 words. The way to improve this is to type in your own convention, such as *car NEAR/15 manufacturers.* That will give you your two words within 15 words of each other.

NESTING

These commands can be used with each other. This is called nesting. Nesting allows you to search within very specific parameters. For instance, you

SAVING NANOSECONDS

If you really want to save time then learn the commands that replace Boolean:

AND	&
OR		
NEAR	~
NOT	!

There, that should save you a nanosecond or two but it might be necessary if you really are in a tearing hurry.

might like to find out more about *investments AND (Georgian silver OR glass)*.

Or you might need information on pets but you have enough information on dogs and tarantulas – so you would type in *pets AND (NOT dogs OR tarantulas)*.

Or you might need to limit your search to specific items with a subject. Let's say you needed to know about carburettors and specifically Zenith and Webber but you weren't too bothered about the rest. Then type in *carburettors AND (Zenith OR Webber)*.

Boolean, by the way, is named after Mr Booles who invented it.

Boolean searches work by allowing you to substitute one word for another without having to search twice

II

LEAVE A SPACE FOR MR BOOLES

Make sure that when you are typing in Boolean commands you leave a space between the words. Thus it should be *car NOT Ford*, rather than *carNOTFord*.

II

UPPER-CASE BOOLEAN

Some search engines require you to type in Boolean commands in upper case. Others are less specific. If you always type them in upper case, you will not fail. If you type them in lower case, you may have difficulty with some search engines such as Excite.

Some search engines require you to use their advanced search facilities. You will see this as a box to click on within their home page.

WILDCARDS

You can search for variations or plurals of words using what are known as wildcards. A wildcard symbol is usually * or sometimes *.* and these symbols, especially the first, are used by all major search engines. Wildcards work by replacing the ending of words or pluralising them. For instance:

POOR SPELLING

If you are not sure how to spell a word but you think you know the beginning then type in what you know and add the $ symbol. For instance you might need to research Boolean commands but have forgotten how to spell Boolean. You know it begins with *bool,* so type that in and add the $ symbol: *bool$.* Your search engine will fill in the blank for you. This may not work with all search engines but it certainly does with Lycos. Don't try this with common words or you'll get a whole lot of pages thrown at you.

- ▶ Type in *danc** and the search will throw up dances, dancing, dancer.

- ▶ Type in *theat** and the search will expand to theatre and theater (UK and US spelling variations).

- ▶ Type in *exhaust** and you'll get exhausted, exhaustion, exhausting.

With some search engines you don't have to do this as they support what is known as stemming; they already give you all the variations you're likely to want. You may have to turn stemming off by using maths or Boolean (we've already covered that!) in order to reduce the number of results to a manageable level.

Wildcards work by replacing the ending of words or pluralising them

TURN OFF FRAMES

If a website gives you the option of turning off frames then do so. Frames take longer to load and serve no useful purpose if you are looking for text-based documents only. Frames are the windows that surround extra documents that you may see on the screen and can be scrolled up or down without affecting the main document.

Bear in mind that some newsgroups don't take too kindly to being used for your own research in this way. If you need to access a newsgroup for research another time, it is best to give yourself time to lurk there for a while until you have acquainted yourself with their conventions and also checked out their FAQ pages — just in case what you want to know has already been answered.

Newsgroups are not there to provide you with answers and might react badly to you if you barge in and demand information. Best to tread lightly and seem genuinely interested, or you might be 'flamed' — sent rude messages by lots and lots of people. And don't 'spam' newsgroups — send lots of newsgroups the same message. They will spot this at once and flame you for your cheek.

Subscribe to any of the online research magazines such as the *CyberSkeptics Guide*, which you can find at: http://www.bibliodata.com/skeptic/ and this will keep you up to date on all avenues of Internet research.

Newsgroups are not there to provide you with answers and might react badly to you if you barge in and demand information

5 verifying facts

OK, you've now collected as many facts as you need to add to your report or proposal or presentation. But just hold on a moment. Just because you got them off the Internet doesn't mean they are accurate, genuine, reliable or up to date. And just because you read something in a newspaper or journal doesn't make it true or trustworthy. At some point someone somewhere is going to ask you to justify these facts – and won't you look daft if you are proved to be wrong?

Best to check quickly that what you are putting in is accurate. You may think you've not got time for this but you will look foolish if someone asks you to verify any data you've presented and you can't or quote sources that can't be checked.

There are four key factors to checking that what you are getting via the Internet is good and useful:

- ▶ **Accuracy**
- ▶ **Authenticity**

- ▶ **Ageing**
- ▶ **Accessibility**

ACCURACY

There are no checks on the Internet. No one supervises the information being posted. No one looks after accuracy in any way, shape or form. There, now you know. There is simply no way, to verify that what you are getting is accurate. There is no editorial control as there would be if you were writing a medical textbook or a law journal. However, discrepancies can creep into both of those.

An example of how lax the Internet is is that of copyright law. There is a lot of information posted on the Internet about such a complex subject. To which country does it refer? Is it the same for all countries? (No, of course not.) Is it accurate? (No, it isn't.) It has been estimated that some 90 per cent of copyright law on the Internet has been found to be incorrect. Don't try it out in a court of law.

But don't panic. There are ways you can verify data quickly and effectively:

- ▶ Collect facts from several different sources if you have time. Compare them. Are they telling you the same thing? If they are then chances are they may well be accurate.

- ▶ Do a quick telephone check with a known expert in the field. If they say it is so, then it probably is so. You may

Just because you got them off the Internet doesn't mean they are accurate, genuine, reliable or up to date not get them to provide you with all the data in the first place but they may be happy to verify what you've got.

► Check the site you are getting the information from – see later in this chapter.

AUTHENTICITY

Technically, the Internet is subject to international law regarding misrepresentation, libel and codes of advertising. However, getting anyone into court is another matter indeed. Sites may look good and appear to be quite genuine but may not be all they seem. For example there are a lot of drug companies running 'anonymous' health sites which appear to give independent and unbiased advice or the results of clinical trials which you would think to be authentic. But are they? Checking the domain name (such as

thinking smart

CHECKING THE DOMAIN OWNERSHIP

Every domain name – the web address or URL – has to be 'owned', registered to someone somewhere. If you go to a domain register site such as DomainRegister.com, you can carry out a simple search of who the website you are using is registered to. This may throw up some interesting stuff you wouldn't have thought of. All you have to do is type in the URL and the register site will tell you the 'real' owner unless they have covered their tracks pretty carefully.

sugarisreallygoodforyou.com) doesn't tell you anything.
So what do you do?

- (▶) Check that any facts collected come from reliable sources and verify them with reference books (if you've got time), experts and your own common sense. Check with other sources and look for the origin of the web page (see 'What's in a name?' later in this chapter).

- (▶) Check with electronic versions of newspapers and journals – these will have been through some editorial process before they appear online.

AGEING

Websites have no start date on them so you have no way of knowing how old they are or whether the information has been updated recently or has sat there twiddling its thumbs for the past three years. Some websites change almost every day and you'll never keep track of the information. What you obtain may be almost out of date before you've even entered it into your report. Obviously for some data, such as who ran the first four-minute mile, this won't be true – but what about stock market prices? Or how about population figures, which change by the minute. You may not need to verify data like these at all, which is lucky for you – saved yourself some more time.

What do you do about this?

> Often on a website there may be a message saying 'last updated 23/9/00' or 'updated every Wednesday'. Check that that has been done – or if it hasn't been updated for a long time you might be best abandoning this site at once unless it contains the sort of data which do not need updating. If there's no message referring to its last update, the chances are it hasn't been done in a while.

ACCESSIBILITY

How accessible are the facts to anyone else who may want to verify them? You should quote your sources but go beyond this and make it easy for anyone else to access them also. Tell your audience or readers where the information is, give them the website address and the page number if relevant. Help them find their way around the site if you have to. Also bear in mind that websites close down, become inoperative at times and change their address from time to time. Print out your data as well, along with any help you can give for someone else to find their way there.

And how about you? You may find the site you want, and you may know the information lurks there, but it is simply buried in so much data that you can't find it. What can you do about this?

> Learn to speed-read (see the next chapter) so you can quickly scroll down the page looking for useful information without having to read every word.

USE YOUR BROWSER

On your browser you will find – along the top – a drop-down menu marked **edit**. Drop this down and you will find a box marked **find in page** [find (on this page) in Internet Explorer]. Click on this and a small browser will open up into which you type your key word/s, and this will seek out, in the web page, what it is you want to find. This speeds up your search considerably and can be used for as many web pages as you've got open without your having to retype your keywords each time.

FILTERED DIRECTORIES

Search engines are run by computers, which means the spiders they use aren't intelligent. They are told to look for keywords and they come back with them. That's all they do. There is no attempt to judge the information for reliability or authenticity. Directories, however, are chosen by human beings and are 'filtered' for out-of-date information, irrelevant sites, wrongly selected sites and sites which are to a greater degree what you are looking for. These filtered directories also give ratings to the sites as to how much pertinent information they contain. If they say a site is 100 per cent then there's lots of information on your keyword search. If they reduce this to 25 per cent, you know there's

Tell your audience or readers where the information is, give them the website address and the page number if relevant probably not a lot of point even looking at that site as the level of information that is pertinent has dropped off. For filtered directories try:

- **Magellan**
- **Excite**
- **Clearinghouse**
- **About**
- **Britannica.**

IDENTIFIED SITES

Look for sites which you know you can trust more than others. Any sites posted by professional institutes are likely to be much more reliable than commercial ones. Same goes for government sites and universities. Trade bodies are usually reliable, as are electronic versions of well known publications, newspapers and journals. Don't be taken in by the domain name alone. Many domain names which sound impressive are used by commercial sites to fool you into thinking they are much more prestigious than they really are.

INSPECT THE WEBSITE

Before trusting a website take a good, long, hard look at it. Ask these questions:

- **Is it updated regularly?**
- **Is it run in a professional manner?**

- ▶ **Is it well written and logical?**
- ▶ **Is it well organised?**
- ▶ **Is it clear and well presented?**
- ▶ **Does any information it has cite sources and references?**
- ▶ **Is there a clear indication of who owns the site?**
- ▶ **Is there a contact address or e-mail address?**
- ▶ **Are there any links to other similar sites?**

If the answer to any or all of these is no, then move on to other sites which can answer yes to most, if not all, of them.

WHO PAID FOR THE SITE?

Websites cost money to put up and run. Someone somewhere is paying for it. Ask yourself why. Ask yourself if there is some catch. Are they trying to sell you something? If the site relies on advertising, they may be getting their running costs from that. If there is no advertising then someone is paying for it themselves and you have to ask why. You have to look for the hidden agenda.

Any website should fulfil certain fundamental criteria if it is to be of any use to you:

- ▶ **The site's purpose should be clear and that purpose should be reflected in its content.**
- ▶ **Sites should contain data, not the opinions or views of the person managing the page – the web master.**

- The advertising on the site shouldn't overshadow the content of the site.

- The information should be easy to access.

- It should be easy to move around the site.

- The site should load (appear on your screen in its entirety) in a reasonable amount of time.

- The information should be updated where appropriate and a last-update date be given.

- The website should be accessible at all times and not subject to constant shutdown for redesign (you want your audience or readers to access it if necessary to confirm your data) – stability of the site is important.

WHAT'S IN A NAME?

Quite a lot, actually. Once you've found your website you need to know how reliable the information is, and this means checking the top-level domain name. This is the bit that comes after the domain name. Let's look at Jertain.com. Jertain

thinkingfast

SAVE AND PRINT

If you don't have time to read an entire document carefully then simply save it for reading later or print it out for later. This frees you to continue searching. Also, reading from the printed page is a lot quicker than trying to read vast documents on screen.

is the domain name and .com tells you it is run by a commercial company – this is its top-level domain name. There are five main top-level domain names (apart from .co, which is the same really as .com):

- ▶ **.edu for educational sites such as universities**
- ▶ **.gov for government sites**
- ▶ **.org for non-profit-making sites**
- ▶ **.com for commercial sites (and .co.uk or .co.au etc., depending on what country it is)**
- ▶ **.net for technology-related commercial sites.**

There are other top-level domain names being currently suggested but as yet they haven't been introduced.

QUOTING YOUR SOURCES

It makes sense if you are including data in a report or proposal or in a handout at a presentation to quote

thinking smart

LOOK FOR THE TILDE

If a web address contains the tilde symbol (~), it means that the name following the symbol is a personal name. These are personal web pages stored on a commercial server and, as such, are probably best avoided because they tend to contain one person's opinion.

your sources. This leaves the reader or audience free to check them if they want to themselves. Remember, though, that you are trying to prove a point, make a case, swing an argument – not necessarily to justify or verify a fact. The fact is there to back up your argument, not as a standalone.

If the Institute of Marketing says that a recent survey indicated that seven out of ten people preferred to shop online then that should be good enough for your audience or readers. You can quote this source with some confidence and don't have to worry too much about 'proving' it. You can quote the data, quote the source and allow anyone to check it themselves if they want to.

If a personal web page says that seven out of ten people prefer to shop online then be much more wary about either quoting it as a 'fact' or using it as a source. After all, if you write in your presentation that Joe Bloggs says seven out of ten people prefer to shop online, what do you expect your audience to think?

By now you should have not only found the facts you wanted but probably been inundated with them. Too many facts can be as daunting as too few. In the next chapter we will look at ways of speeding up the process – finding ways to prune all those data and updating your hardware to make it quicker and slicker to collect and process facts. And after that we'll look at ways of getting you up and out of the office to extend your search out into the real world.

Make sure you are using reputable websites which you have had the time to check for authenticity and reliability. When you can, take some time to check them for other related links, as you'll find that sites which are linked are more reputable than ones which aren't. Check back with sites from time to time, especially if they are useful for research purposes, to make sure they are updated regularly.

Try to stay abreast of Internet development. Such things as top-level domain names change from time to time and the smart manager knows about these changes before they take place and can take advantage of them.

Keep track of where you are getting information from by bookmarking (favourite in Internet Explorer) the sites. This makes it a lot easier to go back to them when you need them. Edit your bookmarks from time to time to keep them fresh and up to date.

If you do lose a site and didn't bookmark it then go to the top of your browser to **tools** and drop down the menu marked **Communicator**. Within this you will find another menu marked **tools**. Click on this. In here you will find a menu marked **history**. In Internet Explorer, click on the history button on the toolbar. This will give you a list of every web page you've visited for the last few weeks. Simply click on the web page you thought you'd lost to be miraculously transported there.

You can reset this history page to keep information for as long or as short a time as you want.

finding facts in an evening

If you have relatively few facts to pull together for your proposal, report or presentation, having a whole evening might look like a breeze. But suppose you need to find lots of data. Or maybe they are just very hard to track down. How do you handle finding facts when the time pressure is really building up?

Clearly you simply can't do as much in half a day as you can in a whole day or more. So the key question is: which bits do you leave out? Here are a few tips for digging up data at the double:

▶ Remember your objective (pages 12–16). Only search for information you *really* need.

▶ Restrict yourself to looking for data from the fastest sources you can. You simply can't afford to waste time scouring the building for the one remaining copy of a five-year-old report that you're not even certain will contain what you want. Broadly speaking, stick to the phone (including your modem).

- Don't even start on facts you aren't confident you can verify. The second you can see that a website, for example, may contain doubtful information, abandon it. Find the information elsewhere.

- If you're working into the evening, be sure you make all possible phone calls first, before everyone goes home.

- The Internet gets very busy in the evenings and at weekends. If you can't use it first thing, you may be better off using it really late. If you're at panic levels watching data download at the rate of a snail with a hangover, just go to bed early, get a few hours' kip, and go back online at four or five in the morning. It'll be much quieter.

- If you've got any friends with faster equipment than yours for accessing the Net, don't be shy. Call round with a generous bottle or two of really good wine and ask them if you can borrow it for the evening. (The wine's for them.)

Go back online at four or five in the morning. It'll be much quieter

finding facts in an hour

Blimey! This is cutting it fine, isn't it? But sometimes there's no choice. Work is piling up around you, or maybe you didn't know you'd need the data until now. Perhaps the meeting you want it for to put your case at has just been pulled forward to this morning. Whatever the reason, don't panic. If you're smart, you can do it. Here's the lowdown:

1 However short of time you are, establish your objective (see pages 12–16). No, I'm not kidding. I know the clock's ticking but this is the only way to do the job effectively and fast, instead of just fast but wrong. There's no point having your proposal or presentation ready on time but so ill-prepared it doesn't convince anyone. You need to identify your objective

because you're going to have to slim down the number of facts you're looking for and this is your magic tool for doing just that.

2 Focus on this objective to decide which points or arguments absolutely have to be included in your meeting, proposal, presentation or whatever it is, and must have factual data to support them.

3 Now go fetch. If you can, delegate the job of finding some (or even all) of this information. But make sure the person you delegate this to understands the argument you are using these data to support.

4 When you're this pushed for time, you have to stay on your toes. You may have to be very inventive about what data you pursue and where from. Who can you call or e-mail who might know? Could you find a different piece of information to make the same point?

5 Don't, whatever you do, succumb to the temptation of using data you can't verify. Just avoid from the start any sources which aren't going to be quick to verify or corroborate once you have the information.

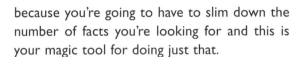

You need to identify your objective because you're going to have to slim down the number of facts you're looking for

The key thing to remember is that it is more persuasive to present a case hinged on three or four core arguments, well supported with verifiable facts, than one based on a dozen or more flimsy, irrelevant or dubious arguments. In other words, when time is tight, focus on quality not quantity of arguments and supporting facts. That should speed things up nicely – *and* make your case far more convincing into the bargain.

It is more persuasive to present a case hinged on three or four core arguments, well supported with verifiable facts, than one based on a dozen or more flimsy, irrelevant or dubious arguments

fast but not now

If you intend to do a lot of serious research – especially on the Internet – then you do need to make sure that the tools you are using are up to date, fast and efficient. There is nothing worse than being in a hurry and having to wait for web pages to download or trying to peer at pages of data on a tiny 14" screen.

UPDATING THE HARDWARE

We all get used to using whatever computer happens to sit on our desk. It may be more than a year old, in which case it simply isn't the most efficient tool on the market. The old adage that computers double in capability and halve in price roughly every year happens to be true. The second you walk out of the showroom with your brand-new RX2000 tucked happily under your arm it's already out of date, as the sales staff had the RX 3000 tucked away waiting until they'd shifted surplus stock of the old 2000 models. Of course they weren't going to tell you. They are there to make a living, same as all of us.

Your computer is a tool, nothing more, nothing less. You deserve to have the best, the latest, the fastest if you need that tool to do your job quickly, efficiently and skilfully. No one would expect a surgeon to operate with blunt scalpels or rusty needles. Yet we are often given old and slow equipment and, therefore, are expected to operate with out-of-date stuff that should have been recycled long ago. Modern computers cost a fraction of what they once did and you can now buy a slick, efficient machine very cheaply indeed.

thinking smart

DON'T SPEAK THE LINGO?

You may well come across sites which are in a foreign language – and they are the very ones you know contain the data you so desperately need. It happens. Don't rush off and learn a new language just so you can read them. Instead try Babelfish. This is a site which will translate for you. It isn't perfect but it will translate whole chunks of text from one language to another. Babelfish is run by AltaVista and will currently handle German, Spanish, Italian, French, English and Portuguese.

MODEMS

If you need to talk to your office manager about upgrading, make sure you have the latest specifications with you – and the justification. If you do Internet research then you need a fast machine capable of handling and processing data in big bites. This means a fast modem – the bit that links your computer with the World Wide Web. Modems were considered fast at 28 kbps (bits per second) a few years ago but now 56 is considered slow and ISDN lines are available. This is a special line that enables very fast connections and fast download times for data. You don't need to know how the technology works. The faster the baud rate (the bps), the better you can get on with your job.

thinking fast

BOOKMARKS

For really speedy research – particularly if you specialise in one or two key areas – you can't beat a decent set of bookmarks. These can be found on your browser. Adding a bookmark is a simple click. Make sure you back up your bookmarks so in the event of a technology malfunction (I hate the word 'crash': it sounds so melodramatic) you can still access them. Update them regularly and delete any you haven't used in a while.

Next you need a machine capable of handling that fast baud rate. And that means junking your old 286 and investing in a proper modern computer that is run by a fast processor – the bit that processes the information. Now, at no point along this journey to improved efficiency and faster work rate do you need to put on an anorak – you simply don't need to become a geek or a nerd.

JUST BUY IT

You don't need to know how anything works – just that it does, and quickly. Go to the showroom and

II **thinking smart**

A WORKING TOOL

Your computer is your working tool. It is there to help you in your search for perfect research to put into the perfect report or proposal. It is not there to entertain you. Delete any games you may have acquired – games are time-consumers. If you need a break or to relax, go for a walk around the office.

Surf the web for research purposes only and save the other stuff for when you get home. Same with e-mails. Tell friends to stop e-mailing you the latest Clinton/Lewinsky jokes. You'll be surprised how quickly you can empty your mailbox when you know it is only work-related items that you're likely to find there.

If you need to talk to your office manager about upgrading, make sure you have the latest specifications with you – and the justification

buy the latest, the best and biggest you can. Make sure it is loaded with the latest software and take it back to the office and get on with it. I know what I said earlier about sales staff but there's no way round it. As soon as you walk out with it I can guarantee you someone will come out with a bigger or faster one at half the price. But don't let this stop you. Buy it and work with what you've got. Update it approximately every 12 months. If you work for yourself, it is tax-deductible and you owe it to yourself to work with the best.

HARD DISK

To process data quickly you need a large storage area – gigabytes of it. No one would expect a filing cabinet the size of a matchbox, so buy as many megabytes as you can. A few years ago 10 or 20

II thinking smart

THE SLEEPING GIANT

Ever noticed that websites take longer to load in the afternoon than in the morning? That's because in the afternoon the sleeping giant awakes – America. Once America wakes up and goes online it clogs up the entire system. You can avoid this by going online when the sleeping giant is still asleep – in the early morning. Yep, you gotta get in the office early.

megabytes was considered extreme, but nowadays software takes up megabytes of disk space in a vast and inexplicable way. You need the most you can get. Believe me, size does matter – at least when it comes to computer storage.

CHECK OUT YOUR BANDWIDTH

You access the Internet via a service (or access) provider. This is a company which gives you your route into the World Wide Web. Some charge for this service and others don't – making their money from advertising. These providers need computers themselves, and the faster, bigger and better they are, the faster and better you can access the Web yourself. You aren't tied to any one provider or limited to only one at any time. Compare their performance by asking about their bandwidth – the rate at which they exchange information with the Web and you – and then choose the best. Ask about modem/user ratios. Once you have seen a few you'll know which is faster and better. The bandwidth is usually measured in bits per second. An A4 page of text is about 15,000 bits, whereas an on-screen video would take about ten million bps to run. You need a server with a minimum of 100 megabytes per second to run such a video and that is about the minimum you'd want anyway. Free

providers operate at around 90, which is considerably slower – this matters when you are in a hurry and need information fast.

SCREEN SIZE

In the old days when computers were clockwork we all sat in front of a 14" screen and thought we were the bee's knees. Today 14" looks positively antique. By upgrading your screen to at least 17" you do two things – first, you give yourself much more room to work in. A big screen can show almost a whole page of A4 without the type being so small you can't read it. Secondly, you can move text around easily – and that text stays fully viewable. It makes sense to go even bigger. A 22" screen will make your working life tolerable in a way you wouldn't believe. Screens aren't expensive – and again are tax-deductible, if you are self-employed.

NETWORKED SYSTEMS

If you work from a networked system then upgrading what's on your desk may simply not be an option open to you. You may be best getting a decent PC or laptop at home and doing your research in the evenings – or, better still, get up early and go online first thing before everyone else does. It's the smart manager who catches the facts.

MIRROR SITES

A lot of popular sites now carry mirror sites. You'll know which ones these are as they will ask you where you want to go to. The American ones always ask 'West Coast or East Coast?' Others will suggest the nearest site to you and others, often the ones where you can download software, will give a list of suggested sites. These are identical but located in different parts of the world. If you are accessing a site which carries a mirror site, look for one which is in a time zone that is least likely to be used. This is usually between 11pm and 7am local time.

So you've updated your modem, screen and hard drive. What about software? Usually this is supplied already installed when you buy a machine, but it too does need updating from time to time. I know we all think software manufacturers only bring out new updates to make us spend money but the updates do improve your working life. If you're still using Word 1 on a 286 with a 14" screen and 64K of memory, don't expect to get any real work done today.

APPLE MAC OR PC?

As for the debate about whether you should go Apple Mac or PC, simply ask yourself what you

If you work from a networked system then upgrading what's on your desk may simply not be an option open to you

thinking smart

WINDWEAVER

Smart managers spend a little time learning as much about the Internet as possible and it makes sense for you to do some homework. A book, even one as slick and as fast as a *Fast Thinking* guide, can only teach you so much. Log on to Windweaver Web Resources for an up-to-the-minute Internet guide which will outline all the search engines with their strengths and weaknesses. This site will also guide you through links and resources. And if you want to go into more academic detail about research, try the Information Research FAQ, which publishes articles relating to a wide range of Internet research.

need your computer for. If you run lots of graphics-based software (pictures) then go for an Apple, but if your data are text-based then a PC is fine. And obviously you need to know who you send files to and receive files from. If your clients or colleagues all use Apples then you might well be advised to go that way. But if everyone around you is using a PC then opt for that.

SPEED-READING

Once you've got all your hardware and software set up there is one aspect of your tool usage that also needs updating – you. There's not much point in having the latest technology importing data fast and efficiently if you can't handle it fast and efficiently yourself. Time for a personal makeover.

Slow readers vs fast readers

We simply don't have the time or space to train you completely in speed-reading. For that you need to invest in a good book on it and a little training yourself. The important thing to remember is that quick readers and slow readers move their eyes differently. Slow readers follow each line from left to right. When they reach the end of a line they go right back to the beginning of the left-hand margin and start again. Fast readers tend to read, or rather glance, down the page keeping their eyes roughly focused on the middle of the page. Fast readers scan, looking for phrases and bits of information that seem pertinent. They miss out all the common words such as 'and', 'the', 'that' and suchlike.

Don't read and drive

A useful analogy is the way police drivers are trained. They don't focus directly on the road ahead but tend to stay slightly unfocused and can thus widen their field of vision. They get to see what is happening at the edges just as much as what is happening in the middle. With a little practice you

You don't need to know how anything works – just that it does and quickly

too can do this — not when you are driving though! Scan the page with slightly unfocused eyes and key phrases and words will seemingly jump out at you.

Waffle and diarrhoea

Some writers, especially if they are using a word-processor rather than a pen or old-fashioned typewriter, have a tendency towards textual diarrhoea. They allow themselves to run on too long and to waffle. Not something, you will have noticed, that happens in a *Fast Thinking* guide. By not reading the waffle and only going for the real bits of information you can speed up the process considerably. If they start to wax lyrical, move your eyes down the page to where they get back to the real meat.

Personal service

Don't expect to do good research if you come back to the office after a large liquid lunch. And similarly if you are tired, stressed or confused, you won't be at your best. First thing in the morning is good for logging on, as you should feel brighter and more enthusiastic. Make sure you are ready to concentrate and are feeling fresh and awake. Take a break every 20 minutes or so just to rest your eyes. Get up and walk around the office. Make sure you sit comfortably and aren't straining your back. Be relaxed and keep your feet firmly on the floor. Research has shown that by keeping your feet flat on the floor you do tend to stay much more alert and upright.

 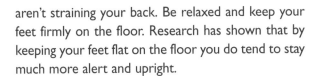

thinking fast

SAVE AND PRINT

When you are reading web pages you can save them and print them out later, which makes them a lot easier to read. Save them as a 'text only' file rather than as an HTML file and you'll be able to open them in a word-processing software package and read them as a plain document – or print them – without all those annoying colours or moving graphics.

for next time

Make sure you stay ahead of the game by keeping abreast of the latest Internet search engines and facilities. You should keep your equipment updated and serviced.

Make sure you do regular back-ups and maintain your bookmarks. Back up your URLs (web addresses) so you know where you got the facts from. If you need them again in a hurry you have easy access to them and, more importantly, your audience can also access them.

By not reading the waffle and only going for the real bits of information you can speed up the process considerably

smart but not fast

Although the Internet may be the fastest and best means of accessing information in this day and age, there are still valuable sources waiting for you outside the office if you have the time to get up and get out there.

TYPES OF INFORMATION SUPPLIER

These can be broadly divided up into two categories – those you have to pay and those you don't. Obviously if you have the time and budget you can simply hand over your fact-finding mission to a researcher and let them get on with it. Perhaps you'd better make a note of this for next time. However, employing a researcher yourself does have drawbacks:

- ▶ You might not get the information you actually wanted.

- ▶ They may waste valuable time and money without any results at all.

A THOROUGH BRIEFING

The key when asking someone else to do research for you is in giving them a thorough briefing on exactly what it is you want – and why, of course.

(▶) **You might get the information you wanted but it might not be in the format you wanted or is perhaps out of date and you'd have to start all over again.**

By the same token, employing a researcher does free you up to get on with life and work, and they should be professional at their job, which could pay dividends. You pays your money and you takes your choice. You could always try an Internet research agency to do your stuff for you. These usually charge a quarterly fee, and the more you pay, the better service you are going to get. Try MindSource, which you will have to access via memo.net.

But if you haven't the time or budget then you're going to have to do it yourself. And this means knowing exactly where to go, how much you want to pay and exactly what you want.

The key when asking someone else to do research for you is in giving them a thorough briefing on exactly what it is you want – and why, of course.

THINKING AHEAD

The smart manager thinks ahead and collects newspaper cuttings (or already subscribes to a newspaper-cutting website), magazine articles, videos and relevant television programmes, and listens to the business programmes on the radio. In general they stay one jump ahead by thinking ahead – you never know when some fact you've collected along the way is going to come in useful.

MARKET RESEARCH

If you need to use market research then you need to know there are various options open to you:

- ▶ **in-depth interviews with consumers**
- ▶ **group discussions among consumers**
- ▶ **at-home product testing**
- ▶ **business-to-business telephone surveys**
- ▶ **brief face-to-face interviews with consumers**
- ▶ **questionnaires**
- ▶ **telephone tracking and attitude interviews.**

They're all different, throw up different views and opinions, and all cost different amounts. Sometimes, someone else may have done the sort of research you need and thus won't have to be

E-MAIL RESEARCH

It doesn't take a moment to e-mail a group of clients, customers, friends or experts to ask quick questions that may throw light on where you should go for information. Your e-mail recipient may already have it. If you don't ask, you won't know. Always ask politely and appreciate that other people may be as busy and as rushed as you are. But surprisingly few people seem to mind being asked and will often spare the time to answer by e-mail, whereas a letter or telephone call may be ignored or the reply delayed.

commissioned to do fresh research but can simply sell you their previous results.

OMNIBUS RESEARCH

You could always combine your research with others. Suppose you needed public opinion about a couple of things. Commissioning your own survey of a couple of hundred thousand people would be frightfully expensive. But if a research company is already going out there asking questions, it is a lot cheaper to add your couple to theirs. This is called omnibus research. Most market research agencies will have details.

Employing a researcher does free you up to get on with life and work but the information you wanted might not be in the format you wanted

TAKE A MOMENT

The smart manager always takes a moment to consider the type of facts they are researching before rushing off to their usual source. A quick trip to a library may save you a lot of wasted time surfing the Internet for information that hasn't yet been posted or might never be posted.

LIBRARIES

These are usually free but you may have to pay for photocopying, and also watch out for the old copyright trouble. I was once refused permission by a librarian to photocopy a page from a book I had written myself! And don't just think in terms of public libraries – there are also university libraries and company libraries.

A quick trip to a library may save you a lot of wasted time surfing the Internet for information that hasn't yet been posted or might never be posted